Playing
With
Patterns

Really Relaxing Colouring Book 1

First published in 2015 by Kyle Craig Publishing

Text and illustration copyright © 2015 Kyle Craig Publishing

Editor: Alison McNicol

Design: Julie Anson

ISBN: 978-1-908-707-03-1

A CIP record for this book is available from the British Library.

A Kyle Craig Publication

www.kyle-craig.com

www.ingramcontent.com/pod-product-compliance
Lightning Source LLC
Chambersburg PA
CBHW080133240526
45468CB00009BA/2408